# Marriage Keys for Crash-Test Dummies

# Marriage Keys for Crash-Test Dummies

Frank T. Williamson

Copyright © 2009 by Frank T. Williamson.

Library of Congress Control Number:     2009904966
ISBN:          Hardcover                978-1-4415-3927-4
               Softcover                978-1-4415-3926-7

All rights reserved. No part of this book may be reproduced or transmitted in any form or by any means, electronic or mechanical, including photocopying, recording, or by any information storage and retrieval system, without permission in writing from the copyright owner.

The names used in this little adventure were fabricated to protect the not-so-innocent. Also, before attempting to crash head-on into the brick wall, please consult an experienced, professional stunt-car driver (or should one say a marriage counselor?).

This book was printed in the United States of America.

**To order additional copies of this book, contact:**
Xlibris Corporation
1-888-795-4274
www.Xlibris.com
Orders@Xlibris.com
62666

# Contents

Acknowledgments ................................................................. 9

Introduction ........................................................................ 11

Words of Wisdom, Dummy: Start with Good Directions ............... 15

Unconventional Wisdom, Dummy:
Get Extended Warranty Insurance Coverage ............................. 27

Some Perks, Dummy: Ensure Good Gas Mileage ........................ 39

Fuzzy Math, Dummy: How Many Miles Ahead? ........................ 49

There Is Graffiti on the Wall, Dummy:
Warning Signs, Sirens Are Flashing ......................................... 57

Wrong Route, Dummy: Potholes Are Waiting Ahead ................... 67

Use Navigational System, Dummy: Clear Traffic Ahead? ............. 74

Fog Lights on, Dummy: Can You See Now? ............................... 81

Ready, Crash Dummy? Are Your Seat Belts Fastened?
Air Bag? Check Check ........................................................... 88

Final Crash-Test Results and Report ........................................ 96

# Dedication

This little adventure is dedicated to all who want to prosper in their relationships with the ones they love. My hope is to elicit positive thoughts that will enable opening of hearts and minds of all who desire to embrace it. Marriage interactions sometimes can become unconventional, thus leading to destruction – consider this adult play, don't let it become child's play:

*Unconventional Marriage Play – "Rock, Paper, Scissors"*

*Rock* – (Wedding Ring),
*Paper* – (Marriage Certificate),
*Scissors* – (Divorce Decree),
The odds of losing in this innocent (but serious) proposition
Increases 50 percent of the time upon marriage commencement
Why take part in this endeavor if one doesn't intend to win?
For crushed lives and painful incisions
Result from rightful or wrongful decisions
Will one fall on his or her own sword? –
Yet waiting and sitting on high is the master
Who will judge and render verdict on the guilty.
Will the one who disavowed the vow,
Get to bow in front of the creator;
If he or she didn't make it right somehow? –
He wants to say,
"Well done, good and faithful servant."
Will you allow him?

"Choose to prosper and stay connected. It can bring many rewards and blessings!"

# Acknowledgments

I have been fortunate to have many people (too numerous to mention individually) who inspired me to craft this little adventure. By no means have they all been positive influencers though. Even the negative ones must be given due because they enabled perseverance and fortitude that assisted in my overcoming of faintheartedness during trying times. They actually helped one to discover life's true meaning and purpose through the pain knowingly and sometimes unknowingly inflicted. Nevertheless, I'm humbly grateful. Even the oyster needs an irritant to create a beautiful gem. As it has been said before, "All is well that ends well." Yes, one's creator does produce beauty for ashes!

"Don't stay with bitterness when joy is right around the corner. Hello, joy!"

# Introduction

This little crash-test dummy manual takes a humorous poke at the institution of marriage. Its intent is not to degrade marriage but hopefully to cause pondering of thought so that one might catapult over a wall (although intangible) that oftentimes blocks marital fulfillment. This perceived barrier seems to be constructed brick by brick with each unresolved marital issue or conflict, and many are crashing head-on, causing traumas too great to recover from. Crashing into it not only hurts physically, emotionally, and spiritually but also ruins lives in the process. The consequences of unhappy marriages, separations, and divorces produce disastrous injuries, which could have been avoided in some cases by slight adjustments in reactions to these marital situations.

Is your marriage so new that you don't envision a wall being constructed let alone ever crashing into one? A wall is constructed one brick at a time. When might your wall have begun to be built? With what was said or done by your partner that you didn't fully comprehend or communicate about? Come out of the clouds for a second, you who are in a love-haze fog, still basking in the warm afterglow of your honey-over-a-moon frolic to wonderland. You too can be clued in to what can go wrong in a marriage that's not made divorce proof.

Or, maybe, you've been married for quite some time and things are going great; everything is on cruise control. Well, take notice too. Whether a divorce looms is not predicated on marriage longevity or wedded bliss. It strikes oftentimes without warning, always looking for the right entry point into a cracked marriage armor. Don't fall asleep at the wheel. Pay attention to the road up ahead.

Lastly, maybe your marriage is rocky, imploding right before your eyes. Maybe you detonated the explosive and the bricks of the wall came crashing down. You said, "What the heck?" rendering inoperable your once-thriving marriage. Is the debris now causing too many hazards? Impairing your vision and stymieing maneuverability? Well, it may behoove you to quickly reassess the situation, start a process to pick up the shattered pieces, and clear a path of those detrimental elements that block marital harmony.

Here's the key premise to start recovery: Foremost, marriages need to be crafted as intended by the creator of them – Psalm 127:1 says, "Unless the Lord builds the house, its builders labor in vain." Really, that is the master key that can unlock the door to so much wisdom and freedom. Are you tired of laboring in vain and crashing into a brick wall? Feel like you're going insane in your marriage? Well, grab the right key, start your engine, and take a test-drive to see if you can avoid the dreaded brick wall. Unless, you enjoy being a crash-test dummy!

This will be interesting . . . Let's go. *Vroom!*

The following are telltale signs that your marriage may be in jeopardy, dummy ("hazardous roadblocks"):

1. He/she takes more walks with the dog than with you.
2. He/she is engulfed in hobbies that more times than not don't include you.
3. He/she spends more time with friends than you.
4. He/she can't seem to find your bed at night without help.
5. TV stands for "too vogue." You can't get enough of watching it instead of your spouse.
6. Money talks louder than your spouse and you hear it.
7. Work is your only outlet.
8. Every opposite sex looks better than your spouse.
9. Nothing is on his/or her ring finger.
10. And lastly, everything seems perfect!

"Make *google* eyes at each other.
Search for directions if you're lost."

# Words of Wisdom, Dummy: Start with Good Directions

Oftentimes, marriages are begging for direction, but no one wants to grab a road map. Where do you need to go? Where do you want to go? Well, one should look for and flag key destinations on a marriage road map and visit some intriguing points of interest. Make sure you both agree to explore, and be open to some exciting opportunities.

Try each key below to start that sluggish engine. One might encounter pivotal marital insight. Does smooth travel on the marriage highway await you? Or will you not follow good directions and crash repeatedly into a brick wall? Remember to park your car and to rest in the best locales when necessary.

*If you want to be treated like a king or queen, get on your throne!*
Do not just expect things to happen by the nature of your position or rank in the marriage. If you want to be treated like royalty, then act that way. Put on your crown, clown!

*Be a role model for your kids. Let them see a marriage that is functioning effectively.*
Quit spawning dysfunctional patterns of behavior for generation after generation to mimic. The world would be a much better place if you (parent) would uphold your end of the marital vow. Act now, not later, for your kid's sake.

*TV dinners are better than TV shows?*
A spouse says, "TV dinners again?" The other says, "June Cleaver always had a nice meal prepared on the table for Ward Cleaver." So what? "Don't leave it to Beaver" and buy into the world's stereotypes. Do get a grip on reality and understand that you can't allow Hollywood's view to dictate the nature of your marriage. A beaver will devour that wood quickly! Be prepared to adjust accordingly. Each one has to carry varying workloads to make the marriage successful. In an instance, get it done, son.

*Oh Lardy, the devil's trying to crash your wedding party? You're going to melt like butter; it's getting hot in here!*
Future mom-in-law wants to rearrange the chairs, the whole family just glares. The girls got mismatch shoes, and the boys got the wedding blues. Too many fingers in your punch bowl; don't panic but remember your goal: get them out before it gets old. Drink the punch dummy while it's fresh, and breathe slowly while counting your guests (or your blessings). 'Cause right now, it's an event!

*Don't bite off more than you can chew. Do buy a starter home.*
No more singing, "When the moon hits your eye like a big pizza pie, that's amore!" Love can't pay the bills. Manage to manage your expectations. Don't crimp your love by creating money pressures. Do not step out on a dead limb. It will give way, and you and your loved one will come crashing down to earth. Before you get hitched, don't land in a ditch, Richie Rich.

*Is your marriage yesterday's news? Then go make raving headlines!*
Today, you can choose to make something good or bad happen in your marriage. You are in control of your future wedded bliss. Why not start with a passionate kiss. A flashbulb by a roving reporter's camera might capture the moment. How cute is that photo!

Are you still following me? I'm trying to get you somewhere. Make sure that you're not distracted drinking coffee and trying to drive. Put that cup down. Keep driving; pay attention. I'll get you there in one piece, I hope.

*Play amateur psychiatrist during the courtship?*
Yes, you can! Did he stay on the couch with remote in hand during your courtship? Chances are he'll be there during your lovely marriage. You should have talked him through a few things when he was lying on your sofa. You knew he was a loafer. He never wanted to be your gofer.

*Dummies are wedding crashers when driving faster to get to the chapel. "Going to the chapel and we're gonna get married." Slow down, don't screech the wheels.*
Eloping can be doping like ball players on steroids. Quick-performance fixers are not the right elixirs. They will catch up with you in the end. Take time to think about a decision that can land you in a marriage prison—dummies busting bricks, taking their licks. This can be hard labor folks.

*Before marrying your future spouse, always remember* rule number 1. *First, attend his or her family reunion. Yes, you, chummy dummy.*
What's in that bloodline? Fruits don't fall too far from the same tree. You might discover some rotten apples on the ground at that family picnic. You don't want to bite on those, do you? Hmmm.

*Take the* M *out of money and replace it with* H *and your marriage will be sweeter! Money really can't buy love.*
Money problems have wrecked the best of marriages – even when there was plenty available. Try too much honey instead; it can get sticky, but it will cause lovesickness. I prefer that – yummy!

*Always make the most of life's second chances.*
If you make a mistake and are able to live for another day, then by all means learn from it. Do not repeat the same error; it will only cause undue terror.

*Inspire; do not deprive. The kid(s) will remember.*
Got little ones? Have a family talent show and reward each for the show of his or her talents no matter how great or small. Understand that you are shaping a life. Positive affirmation can propel a child to dizzying heights. Give each one a fair chance and watch them dance!

*Get some instruction to prevent destruction! What do I do? Not now, wait to recite your wedding vows, dummy.*
If you're not in shape to drive the car, then catch the train. Huh? You want to make your wedding, "the occasion." So grab the train so that the bride doesn't go insane! Get someone to hold up the end of her beautiful gown or you'll end up in the dog pound. Do as you're told and make a joyous sound. *Choo! Choo!* The train is about to arrive at the station (or altar).

*A reminder in case you forget or don't know any better: another man's (or woman's) junk is another man's (or woman's) treasure.*
Open the gift of your spouse. Discover the treasures inside. Something had to intrigue you for you to offer your marriage proposal. Do not flounder by keeping your treasure chest locked and dusty. Open it today. Explore and go fishing for something, fool.

"Oh, for goodness' sake. Don't fish while I'm driving. You're going to get that hook in my leg, baby."

*Love your spouse, not your home, car, job, clothes, or jewelry. Inanimate objects don't deserve love.*
How could you profess your love to him or her and then spend all your time loving toys that will never satisfy? Love your wife for life (ditto, wife to husband).

*God created man in his own image. Quit trying to give him a bad view of his creation by misbehaving.*
I can only imagine the creator saddened by all the pollution in the world. Not to mention the convolution of his marriage institution. Clear the air over there. Now inhale deeply. And enjoy!

*Cinderella, where's your fella? He's waiting for you loyally just like old yeller.*
You walk down the aisle while all admire your beauty, but your beau is looking rather slo-mo with those puppy eyes. You've prepared a celebration to astound, but he looks like a hound out of bounds. Grab your honey; let him know he's stunning. Remember to include him in this special day lest he howl at the moon come judgment day! Do you want to end up with a wolf?

*Commit to each other for life.*
Contrary to popular belief, love is not a feeling; it's a commitment. Question: if it was raining outside and there was no sun shining, do you give up on life because of that stormy day? No, you get the proper gear and brave the elements. Go to work. "The sun'll come out tomorrow, bet your bottom dollar that tomorrow there'll be sun." Together, write a plan for your marriage, or you'll fail to plan for success.

*Is she a "hottie?" Then beam her up, Scottie.*
When God created Eve for Adam, he took the rib out of Adam and made her. A rib is a beam to support the house. If it's not there, the house will fall. I guarantee. Allow the beam to be erected, and the house can be perfected.

*In marriage, it is mature not manure. Don't stink up your house with immaturity.*
Yes, the marriage needs some fertilizing; but by golly, no need to seed it with folly. Get out some perfume or cologne, and spritz, baby, spritz. Smells delightful!

*Man, a pedicure is definitely in store. Otherwise, she might ignore the knock at the hotel door.*
"It's your wedding knight, baby, I'm ready."
"Okay, I hope you're ready. Oh no, you got to walk this way, buddy! Put them in a tub and scrub." Smooth feet, too, are a girl's treat. She doesn't want your hoofs to tear the satin sheets! My goodness, dummy.

We've gone a few places, done a few drive-bys. The directions are good. Now let's keep going; there are lots of places to see. Having so much fun! *Screech*. Off and running again.

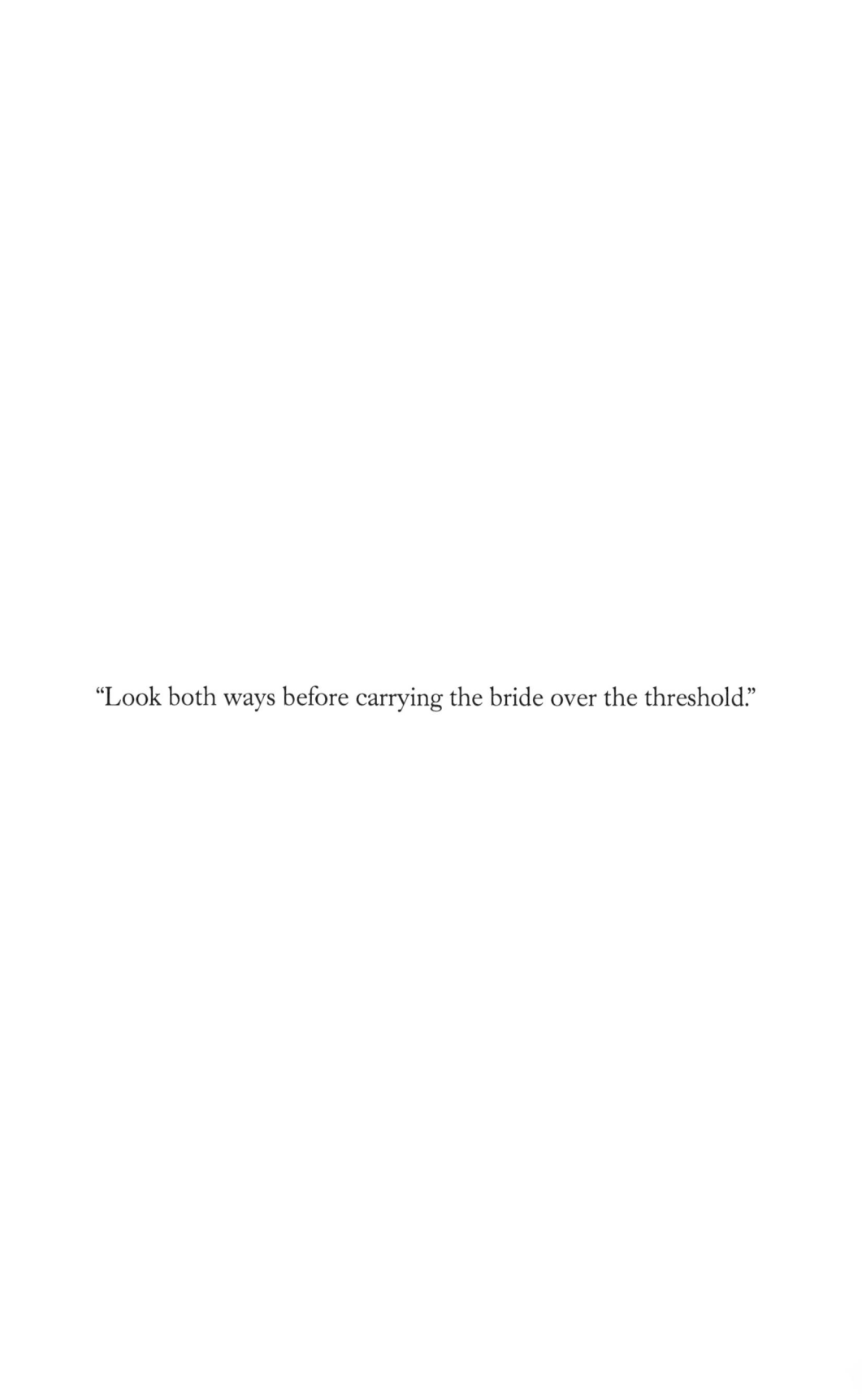

"Look both ways before carrying the bride over the threshold."

# Unconventional Wisdom, Dummy: Get Extended Warranty Insurance Coverage

Marriages come in different colors, shapes, and sizes. If you're going to squeeze into that racing cockpit together, make sure you leave room to think outside of the box. Also, get proper accident coverage. You're sure to encounter some bumps and bruises along the way. It really doesn't cost much to protect your investment. Be wise; get that extra cushion.

*Man, do not get forced into wearing tux tails at your wedding. That's old-school fool.*
Watch out, dude, you'll end up shaking your tail feathers. Have a voice; get into proper position. You are the head; if not, you're dead. Do not just flip a coin and call tails. There is a fifty-fifty chance that you'll lose. If she is the head and you're the tail, the marriage is being set up for failure. Why? You're out of alignment, and disasters are waiting to happen. The man should be the head of the household. "Don't argue with me, girl. Trust me. I won't steer you wrong."

*Make your stake in the marriage sizzle!*
Turn on the heat under that old cast-iron skillet. Add just the right spices, and *voila*! Your marriage won't fizzle, and you'll hear the sizzle. Now sniff and smell that succulent marriage. Tasty!

*Do reinvent the marriage wheel.*
Spin the wheel and see what it lands on. Don't be afraid to try something new. If you've ever played spin the bottle and got a throttle, why not spin the wheel and get a thrill! You won't get dizzy, fool.

*Go the extra mile when you're feeling burnt-out.*
Sometimes, you got to try to go farther. Oftentimes, your destination can be reached on that last bit of gas fumes. And then when you do arrive, you can kick your feet up and rest. Enjoy your stay; y'all come back, you hear.

*Allow your spouse to sing off-key once in a while.*
Do not be so constrictive and judgmental. Relax. We all hit a sour note every now and then. Besides, you might even get a good laugh together out of the deal. It is deal or no deal, but you win, friend!

*Are you brain-dead, dummy–comatose in the host? What are you talking about?*
"Feel free to travel the hemisphere, dear. You should use either the right or left side of your brain. Let's travel the world, Earl. Think creatively or logically; the more you try, the better we fly. Open the hood to your cranium and fire up the neural spark plugs." You got to go first class if you want it to last, dummy. Schedule a trip down memory lane; it can do wonders for your brain.

"Make up your mind. Are we driving or flying? Either way I'm going with the flow, honey! Okay."

*When you feel an argument coming, speak softly and carry a big stick of gum to chew on.*
Go ahead. Put the gum in your mouth and chew. Do not get it on the bottom of your shoe. It's a bit messy there. Remain calm; no need for a false alarm, but keep walking cautiously.

*If you can't cook, act like you can.*
Remember when you made mud cakes or mud pies when you were a kid? You pretended that they were scrumptious. Guess what. If you mess up, fess up. You can always make a second batch.

*Ignite something to start a fire.*
Has your marriage lost its spark? Then rub together, you two stones! Do not just look at each other stone-faced. Can't stay in that condition? Find something to revive your ignition. Maybe experience an exciting hobby together? Create something, dummy!

This ride is getting rough. Get over on the left side of the road and speed up, please. Still bumpy? Don't worry; this road will not last forever. Thank goodness. I think we're going somewhere.

*Enjoy the carnival.*
Does your marriage seem like a merry-go-round? Well, sit down, horseplay, and have fun! Get out of that rut. Smell some popcorn and listen to the carnival music. Have a funnel cake through the tunnel of love. Oooh, baby!

*Be careful what you ask for. Huh?*
Is your spouse too *FAT: F*all the *T*ime for you? Then love him or her back. Encourage; do not discourage. Retell a story of "Once upon a time when I met you." End the story with "happily ever after." Are you really envisioning a lifetime together after "I do, boo?"

*Poke a stick at that snake. Oh no!*
Your marriage may be slow, but it's movin'; now start groovin'. Poke a stick at that reptile. It's not dead if it still has its head. Use your noggin to think of something to move that wiggly thing. Get busy!

*Not married and feeling like an old maid? Well, play the card that's dealt to you and enjoy the game.*
A wrinkled card does not get picked in this game when it obviously conveys you badly want to be chosen. So keep yourself and continue to be positive in which you are; go about your life's business and shine your star. When you least expect it, someone will pull your card and be quite surprised of who you really are–a beautiful gift to last by far!

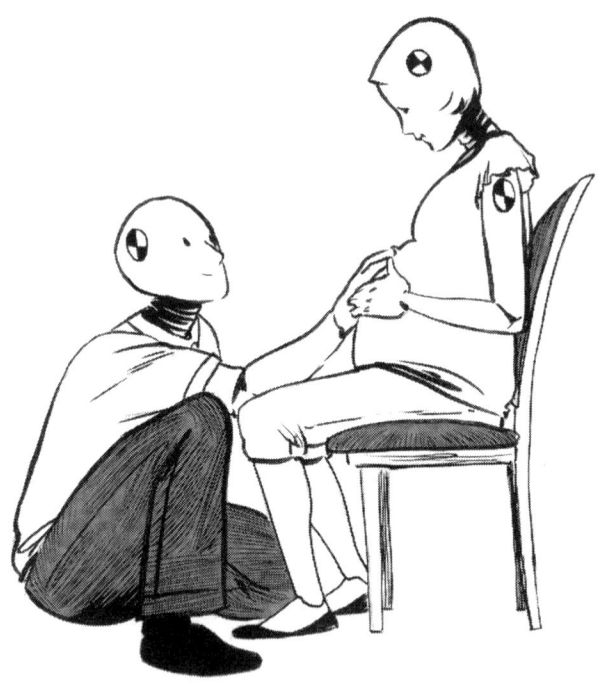

*Ancient experience and wisdom is good? Tell me about that fact, Jack.* Lamaze doesn't have to mean le maze. Great-great-grandma didn't do Lamaze, and she found a way to deliver that baby successfully. Lighten up, girl. Don't stress out when you're incubating your first child. God gave you innate abilities, so use them. He'll help you deliver out of your quiver. "Awh!" Junior done kick you in the liver?

*Get off that couch and get your derriere moving. Give yourself some wiggle room.*
Marriage lip-o-suction: Kiss that hippo-botto-me good-bye. Oui, au revoir! (Yes, good-bye!). Go to a health club and take the pain medicine. Grab a bottle of water. That medicine ball may be hard to swallow and taste bad, but trust me, it will do wonders for you.

*Gut check time: get a grip on your marriage.*
How? Use those love handles for motivation. You want to stay attractive for each other, don't you? So grab the handlebars and ride that exercise bike. You go, boy! You go, girl!

*Put some butter on your toast and enjoy life. What, after all that diet talk? Go right ahead.*
Marriage health gets better when you splurge every now and then. Why not? Feel free to get in the danger zone; go ahead and splatter your toast!

*Get "beagle" advice to protect your assets.*
If you claim to have the goods (got it going on like you think you do?), then get him/her to sign a "pre-pup." Make sure he/she does his/her business on paper. Sign where you're supposed to sign. Also, wean him/her. He/she has got to grow up. He/she should be housebroken and made ready to eat out of his/her own bowl. Sometimes, you gotta be that way with a "newbie."

*If merging families, do so carefully.*
A blended family is like mismatched socks found after laundry. Make sure that you connect the matching pair out there. Try hard to put the proper pieces in the right places, or you won't have a true picture. Make sure your kids know who they are. Do not distort the truth. It can only help their self-worth.

*Make your marriage an anomaly.*
Never mind that everyone else is getting divorced. Set a new standard. Stay together for the sake of the vows that you made before your creator. Where is your honor and commitment? When in doubt, work it out.

We made it safely to another destination albeit slowly, but better late than never. What's next? Let's check our mileage. Enough fuel to ride to the next destination? You bet!

"Your love deserves an encore: play, adore, and explore more."

## Some Perks, Dummy: Ensure Good Gas Mileage

Are you still trying to rev up the engine but going nowhere? Burning unnecessary fuel? Quit putting in that lower-grade octane gas. Knocks and pings won't get you to the next marriage hideaway. Act like you're going somewhere. Press down on the accelerator and go! See you in a bit.

*Get more energy. Recharge your batteries.*
The Energizer Bunny keeps going and going. What's wrong with you? Are you not recharging your batteries? Short-circuiting your efforts? Find something to get charged up about. Find positive ways to pulsate the heart. Love – that's a great start!

*Yo! Get out the Play-Doh. oh?*
Soften up and try to create something. Use your imagination to create elation! Color each other's world with shades of clay. Mold something that'll clear away gray skies. Now get over to your play station, kid at heart. And play!

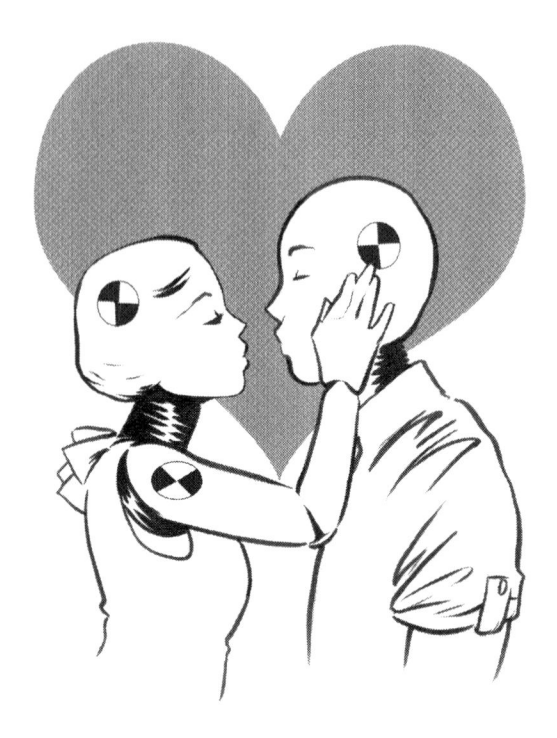

*Feed each other constantly for a healthy marriage.*
Serve your spouse sugar smacks (kisses) for breakfast. They are the breakfast of champions! Breakfast is the most important meal of the day. Also, throughout the day, pucker like a goldfish. There never should be such a thing as too many kisses. Feed your spouse often, but don't get him/her too bloated because he/she won't be able to swim happily.

*Shower flower power and sprinkle fragrances of faith, hope, and love.*
Ah, the smells of those sweet fragrances – fresh as the morning dew! If only you knew how to pick a rose and offer appropriate prose. Don't just stare, try something, do something – silly. Anything!

*Learn a new love lesson–give your dummy a "Painted Smile" poem:*
I painted this smile especially for you,
It was selected with care, faith, and virtue.
My brush dried up many times,
But I wetted with your tears of happiness.
You didn't know that I was into art
But anything I would do to fulfill your heart.
I put the final touches on with precision
Because your love does not show indecision.
So, please, stay with me a while.
Here, have my painted smile.

*Pettiness should not have a place in your relationship. It soils the union.*
Don't gross out. At the end of the day, who cares in what direction the toilet paper dispenses as long as it gets the job done? And does it matter if I squeeze the tube of toothpaste at the top, middle, or bottom? Get smart and buy toothpaste in a pump dispenser. Don't waste time with insignificant things. They will only subtract negatively from the few precious hours in a day.

*Limit your expectations and keep yourself in check.*
Go into the marriage as though Prince Charming and the princess don't exist, and you might be pleasantly surprised. If you offer respect and decency to each other, that frog you kissed might turn into royalty. "Rib bit."

*It's dandy to make your baby your eye candy! Whatcha say, dummy?*
Surround your girl like a peppermint swirl. How sweet! Defy your guy; make him the apple of your eye. It's crème de la crème, get to know him. Get sticky and gooey so you can do it. Whatever works gets you perks.

*Follow a recipe and bake a cake together. Share the beaters that make the batter and your heart might flutter.*

If you can whip into shape some basic marriage ingredients – *sugar* and *flower* – you might just get that cake to rise and some icing to boot. Sweet *toot-toot*! Then you both can enjoy a big slice with some ice-cold milk. Yummy, dummy – oh my tummy!

*Together, grow young at heart. Two hearts can beat as one, son.*
It's all right to hold hands. Quit acting like an old fogy. Every now and then, don't act your age or years in the marriage. You might turn an interesting page in the chapter of your marriage life.

*Get the lingerie back out of mothballs. Why are you sniffing like that, you old geezer?*
What lingerie? Don't hide the lingerie after the first or second child unless you're creative and can color outside the lines. Spice it up for life. Got a pulse? She's alive!

*Get a marriage tune-up. You gotta go long for this pass, baby!*
Two important dos in your marriage – regular oil changes and tire rotations: Attend some marriage classes and seminars. Perfect your timing; it keeps the marriage engine humming. You want it to last for a lifetime, don't you? In the end zone, touch down!

"Uh-oh. Maybe, we should stop this drive?"
"No, not now. We're not even close to being done, sweetie."

*Put more deposits in the marriage bank and make less withdrawals.*
Quit robbing the bank, you bandit. Do not take out everything all at once. Make sound investments to compound the marriage interest. Save for a raining day. It might get cozy inside the vault, Walt.

*Remember that your love should be unconditional. Huh, is it?*
It shouldn't be what have you done for me lately. Life causes us to grow in stages. There is trial and error. Allow room to grow. You should love your spouse greatly, not Johnny-come-lately.

Never *and* always *words shouldn't exist in your vocabulary.*
Do you really believe those words when you say them loosely? Do you have lapses in your memory? I think you do. Look all around for a clue of all the things he/she does for you. Simple and true reflection deserves its due, Gertrude.

*Chivalry still has its place today even though its extinction is often predicted. Protect the species, show acts of courage, dummy.*
Lay down your arms and invite her in. Valor, honor, and courtesy are things she wants to befriend. She can only sway to the music that you play. What sound are you creating? Hopefully, it's in surround (hug her) sound, and she hears beautiful music from any position.

We've made good time and still have some fuel in the tank. Shouldn't have much farther to go; we're still trying to avoid that brick wall though. Got it in our sight; let's keep driving. We'll try to steer clear of it.

"Put your specs on if things remain a bit fuzzy."

# Fuzzy Math, Dummy: How Many Miles Ahead?

We're moving again. Are we there yet? Whoa, slow down. Did I hear your cuckoo clock chime? Oh, you say, "My marriage needs a boost." What happened to that good gas mileage? If you can stay steadily on course, you might avoid some costly miscalculations. You're getting closer to the brick wall, but you just might have enough turbo power. If you can floor this thing, you might scale it. *Vroom!*

*Marriage is too costly not to succeed. Don't break down when you're almost there.*
Rings + ceremony + honeymoon + divorce = broke. Why create all the fanfare if you don't plan on making it work? If you expect your marriage to die, then go ahead and let it RIP! (rest in peace). Better yet, just start with the JOP (justice of the peace). In the end, you just might come out cheaper.

*The divorce rate percentages increase as you move up the scale in successive marriages. Go ahead. Climb the ladder, but watch your steps.*
Some think the odds of success are greater after the first marriage. Think again. You should have learned something from the first one. The next time you marry, make sure that you have all your ducks lined up in a row, or do you enjoy waddling and stubbing your toe?

*Start practicing sound money management.*
Do your wedding rings cost significantly more than that entire pricey wedding ceremony? Now, is that sound money management if your money is funny? Hey, look, I think Benjamin is smirking at you. Ring the Liberty Bell 'cause it's going to be hell!

## "Did I hear a bell?" Yes, school is in session, dummy.

*Marriage math is 1 + 1 = 1. Huh? Is that dummy math or a trick question?* Don't scratch your head. I'll let you figure this "one" out. I'll give you a few seconds. Okay, time's up. I bet you didn't learn that kind of math in grade school. Take off that dunce cap. Get out of the corner. This is marriage math. Are you saying, "Who is going to meet my needs?" Don't be selfish. If you get this math, you are well on your way to acing the test! What one does affects the other.

*Use common cents or sense. Don't wince. What? You're confusing me, smarty-pants.*
"Why do I have to put the toilet seat down? I thought I married a high IQ." Hey, cool fool, it doesn't cost you anything. Just throw a penny for Jenny in that wishing well. "Oh, my bad. I'll try to remember the next time. Excuse me for my thoughtlessness."

*Be responsible. Don't drink and drive the shopping cart.*
His idea of grocery shopping for the family is beer, pizza, and chips. Get out the antacid, please! His idea of money spent on family essentials is money left after a couple of brewskis and golf. Oh no! "I sent you to the grocery store, and you get sidetracked. And to top it off, you placed a bet on your pitiful golf game." That's lame, and the perpetrator shall remain game-less. Mulligan!

*Be considerate. Make your bed and sleep in it.*
Remember, when shopping for apparel for your mate, if you forget or do not know her size, always buy a size smaller than what you think she is. She'll appreciate you for the compliment. Flattery can take you places and help you to avoid sleeping on little sofas and in cramped doghouses.

*Adultery doesn't pay dividends.*
Wondering if that woman over there is taken? Maybe, I could get on with her? Wondering if that man over there is available? He is off the charts on a scale of one to ten. The grass always seems a lot greener on the other side. Maybe it requires more fertilizer, and if the sun gets too hot, that yard can go up in flames rather quickly.

*Think logically. Okay, give me a second. Let me figure this one out.*
There are only two seats in my sports car, and we are a family of three? "Why did I buy this car? I have no place to put the baby's car seat, and I don't have a second car or the money to buy one." I not smart. "Can we put the baby in the trunk?" Dude, have you lost your mind?

*Dummy, you can't take a day off. Marriage is 365 days a year.*
"There you go again with numbers. What about leap year? Am I jumping to conclusions if I crash on that day?" Yes, you are, dummy. Use that extra day to synchronize your relationship. Leap year is done to synchronize the seasons; so why not your marriage relationship. That's a good enough reason. Change can be quite pleasant.

I believe I've had enough I'm getting winded. Let's hurry so I can get out and lean up against that brick wall ahead. "Watch it, sucker!"

"Make a positive mark on your marriage,
make it famous and legendary."

# There Is Graffiti on the Wall, Dummy: Warning Signs, Sirens Are Flashing

Unlike Michael Jackson's *Off the Wall* album during the late 1970s, the graffiti is on the wall. Stop. "Hee, hee." Put on the brakes. *Screech!* It was said that love is color-blind. So why does one somehow see color after the marriage? How can you fall in and out of love? Was it really love? Oh, excuse me, is that what happens when you're blind?

Did you know that you were different before getting married? Ever wondered, if both of you are alike, then someone is unnecessary? You must respect and value each other's differences. In fact, if acknowledged and respected, your differences will enhance the marital experience. Just do not tax the other person with your eccentrics. Time for pause and communication here; however, no time, gotta keep moving, the lights are flashing. Alert, you're encountering some unusual terrain!

*Keep your dress clean and you'll go places.*
Bleach your wedding gown so you can wear it downtown. Huh? Has he proposed to you yet after seven years of dating? Well, the dummy is dragging your wedding gown through the mud. Maybe he's thinking that you're not worth marrying or he's not the marrying kind. 'Cause he would have married you by now and kept your wedding gown – sparkling clean!

*Beware of red flags that appear pink.*
(Hint: she was quite pretty in pink and just too fine.) See beyond the physical. Don't ignore the real red flags (or stop sign) raised during dating. Pink bunnies may play well for Easter, but not for serious cohabitation, silly rabbit.

*Don't paint over the graffiti to clean the smut.*
She goes to church; he goes to bars. Oh no, here comes trouble. Get that speck of dust out of your eye; you can't see clearly. Are you compatible in your morals or values? If you don't share the same beliefs, chances are that you'll share in many griefs.

*Banish the cart-before-the-horse syndrome.*
What came first? The kid or the marriage? You may have a steep hill to climb with the horse trailing the cart that you're pulling. Do you really think you're off to a great start?

*Treat each other with dignity.*
He calls her "my old lady," and she puts him in "the doghouse." Is that respect? Chances are you're taking each other for granted if those terms are being tossed around loosely.

*Got buzz? Be like buzz Aldridge and land on the moon. Moonwalk, dummy, fantasize; even if it's a dummy mission and you can't dance.*
Shoot for the moonlight in your dancing and romancing; you might just land on Pluto. Try something exciting. Wish upon a falling star and you might see stars in her eyes. She may even want to experience your universe!

*Try to support and share in each other's interests.*
She likes to shop; he likes to plop. Go suck a lollipop! Maybe you can go with her and tell her how nice she looks in that dress. You might get caressed.

*Change your mind-set. Positive thinking helps.*
Break the cycle of divorce. Just because your great-grandpa and great-grandma's and Uncle Joe and Aunt Betty's marriages ended in divorce doesn't mean yours will. "Stinkin' thinkin'!"

*Cherish each other, not things.*
She cherishes her doll collection, he his model car collection. What do you cherish about each other? C'mon, you can think of something.

*Dummy, if you bust your windshield, it means something.* "Huh?" *Since you weren't properly strapped in your seat belt good, your head went forward and hit against it.*
The glass fragments can cut off your thinking. "What?" Okay, this is what you do. Take the *d* for dummy out of the windshield. And what you come up with? "Win shield" Keep doing those positive things that will enable your relationship to prosper and block the negative things from damaging it. "Right, I got to replace that windshield." You are a smart dummy.

## "Keep talking. I think I like what I'm hearing."

*Discuss the things that really matter. Get rid of the idle chatter.*
She wants kids; he doesn't. You can't settle for half a kid. So what will you do? Communicate; prepare to deflate that hot-air balloon of idle chatter. It really does matter.

*Strike a balance and negotiate, or prepare to strike a match.*
He is a flea market kind of guy; she is Tiffany's to the rescue. Someone douse this fire with gasoline. Quickly get out, something is about to blow!

*You can't change your partner's habits.*
"We'll change each other." Right, do you really think so? He or she will probably remain an old stiff – dead on arrival. Most likely, you'll change to a new partner before you change the one you're with. Old habits are hard to die, and oftentimes they multiply.

"Did you say dummified?" No multiply, meaning exponentially. Are you on board now? "Yes."

*Dummies don't get henpecked if they stay out of chicken coops.* "You got to be kidding."
No, stay in the boat and drive. "The coop can be amiss if there's no Henrietta regatta?" Yes, let the misses delve into a book on the passenger side while the rooster drives. Cockle-doodle-doo!

I'm trying to shift gears; got to slow this thing down. Too many obstacles up ahead. Let's see what this manual says; I got my checklist. The equipment appears all in place. Spare in the trunk, flares, first-aid kit, and arms and legs are still intact. Good. Okay.

"Some things can seem unsightly until you make them over in your mind."

# Wrong Route, Dummy: Potholes Are Waiting Ahead

Get out the GPS device. Why, do you avoid the scenic route in your marriage? Do you see smog and not clear skies? Oh my! Now swerve over that junk and get off the main road; head for the scenic route just for a second. Take the time to observe the beauty that you once knew. A long, slow pause to view your marriage landscape doesn't quite sync together so well in a fast-paced world, but you really have to take the time. Be careful of the many unsightly and treacherous potholes that can develop on a road that is worn and well traveled. You might avoid a costly breakdown if you seek a different viewpoint or greener pastures, so to speak. Plenty of sunshine up ahead if you just keep driving. Enjoy.

*Tend to your marriage lawn and garden.*
Marriage is like lawn and garden work. Get on your knees and cultivate some ground. Plant the right seeds during the right season. In due time, you will reap a harvest, if you faint not. However, both have to share in the mowing, edging, and pulling of weeds if you expect nice aesthetics and luscious fruit.

*Keep the home fires burning.*
"We barely have embers glowing on this passion." After two kids, she doesn't know what sex is and he doesn't know what it's not. "Oh my, what have we gotten ourselves into?" Figure this out urgently. Practice fire alarms repetitively – date night and special occasions. Get the kids out of the house. Quick!

*Learn what an HOV lane is – "Hang On, Velma"?*
Do not think that you can outrun the police when you're driving illegal in this faster lane. It's easy to recognize two dummies trying to beat the system. Dummy impostors will get pulled over and ticketed on an ill-fated and quick marriage jaunt. Be real when you two buckle that car seat belt.

*Seek a true marriage professional for sound advice.*
Testing 1, 2, 3. Can you hear me now? Get closer. His idea of marriage counseling is he and she sitting at a table with a beer can doing all the talking. Her idea of marriage counseling is she and he watching Dr. Feel Good and Oprah Win Free Cars!

*Recognize an unhappy marriage.*
"Does it **Mar r** Love, and **i** do **age?**" Translation: "Your *marriage* is busted and disgusted?" Hopefully, you don't have to decode it to know that it has gone sour. You get out of it what you put into it. Write a better script so that you won't trip. Fix your lip. Quit sulking, you sourpuss.

*Oh, not now, brown cow! Milking the udders ain't cool.*
Not buying the cow but drinking the chocolate milk? A trial-run subscription doesn't promise a money-back guarantee if not completely satisfied in this game. *Moov* over, and get it right. No milking (sex) tonight. What time is your flight?

*Activate your faith.*
Why are parts of the Bible expressed during the wedding ceremony but left out during the actual marriage years? "Duh. Huh?" Remember the glue that will hold you two.

*Apply what you learn. Practice makes perfect.*
"Should we have separate checking accounts?" (Answer: refer back to fuzzy math, 1 + 1 = 1.) Remember that you are one, but go ahead and have a separate account for each of you to splurge as needed. However, keep that one checking account together for all those important bills. Repetition is good. Keep asking the same questions if you don't understand.

*Have you really looked at your wife lately? Dummy, what do you see?*
Is she the woman in your "dear-view" mirror? You want to see her nearer and dearer so you've got to focus on her completely. Adjust the mirror to see her clearer. Isn't she gorgeous! Take another look.

"Mirror, mirror on the wall, who is the most famous of them all?" Okay, you're getting carried away. Not you, dummy.

"Make your gps a God positioning system. You'll never be lost."

# Use Navigational System, Dummy: Clear Traffic Ahead?

Are we off course? Let's see.

Shouldn't you pull over and ask for directions, dear?" "Remember there is a navigational system in this car, honey?"

Marriages have taken place throughout time. There is so much wisdom to draw upon. If all else fails, at least check another source. (Hint: it is one of the most historically read books and has stood the test of time. Answer: the Bible.) Choose to use it for greater clarity.

*Try odd little things. Mix it up.*
For a prosperous marriage, try throwing long-grain or success rice, not short-grain or minute rice, after the ceremony. Maybe your marriage will last longer. Just a thought; besides, it won't hurt a thing.

*Choose your music wisely; do not play the wrong wedding song.*
Wrong wedding lyrics: "These boots are made for walking, and . . . gonna walk all over you." You're in trouble. You know that, don't you?

*Open your mind to different thinking.*
Maybe the divorce rate is so high because most marriage ceremonies never start on time. If you were constantly late for work, chances are you would end up being fired, wouldn't you? Is that why many marriages end up terminated?

*Try to keep your thoughts and words in line.*
dySlEXia: She says *no,* and he thinks she means it's *on.* Quit getting your words (SEX and EX'S) twisted too.

*Use keen vision to scan ahead for potential events.*
What? His and her vanities? Splitting assets already? Premonition: Something may be looming, sweetheart. "Oh no, not the nasty *D*-word?" Divorce or delusional? Settle down, you're missing something. Regroup, please. It's not that serious.

*Analyze the situation, but don't get caught up.*
Ever wondered if the groom did see the bride before the wedding? He might know what he's getting himself into. Smarty-pants, you're too smart for your own good. You're overanalyzing, quit peeping!

*Get your finances organized.*
"What can we actually afford? Did you hear me, honey?" Budget means "Bud, get it?" It doesn't hurt to itemize your expenses. Though try not to dramatize them.

*Mind your own manners, and everything will take care of itself.*
"Honey, you say that we have to each look at ourselves in our own mirror to correct our problems. But why do you keep peeping over and looking into my mirror? When I see your reflection in my mirror, it distorts everything." Play fair. Do not glare or stare into your spouse's mirror, and you'll see things clearer.

*What's a bride like without her groom? It's like a man without his fruit of the loom.*
No comfort. Also, if a woman or man is without the fruit of the spirit (love, joy, peace, long-suffering, gentleness, goodness, faith, meekness, and temperance), there's no contentment in the relationship. Give your relationship sustenance so that it will bloom. Embrace your groom with sweetness–show him the fruit of the spirit!

"Yeah!  That's delightful, baby."

## MARRIAGE KEYS FOR CRASH-TEST DUMMIES | 79

What mile marker are we approaching? The last leg of this journey is in sight. I just can't wait to get there. Hang on. *Zoom!*

"FOG: Figuring out gals [and guys]."

# Fog Lights on, Dummy: Can You See Now?

"Can't see nothing out here, babe. Slow down. Afraid we're getting close to that wall, dear. Do you have the low beams on?"
"Uh, it is looking weird out here."

*Ask the right questions. And get the right answers.*
"Why don't you treat me like you used to?" Because you don't treat yourself like you used to. If you take better care of yourself, I can take better care of you.

*Resolve disagreements quickly.*
Don't let the sun go down before you put your problems to bed. Don't go to sleep angry and think that it will disappear by morning. Many divorces result simply from unresolved conflict. Yes, hindsight is twenty-twenty. Dummy, you could have made it. Duh?

*Cheer for the right home team. Know your spouse's score.*
His idea of a stork is NBC, "the peacock," carrying a Sunday-night football game. Not her idea, man, you're lost. What about her favorite team? A family is what she craves, not "stork" pigskins. Excuse me, did you say pork pigskins? Gimme some, throw me one. Crunchy!

*Ask questions and reinforce things that are not clear to aid understanding.* She suggests that they have their first kid, and he thinks to himself, I don't know how to raise no goat! "Where is the paper?" Are you saying that you want a divorce, or do you want to feed the goat? Don't be ambiguous.

*Again, get clarity; don't misinterpret.*
She says, "Let's tie the knot," and he says, "On whose neck? I ain't playing hangman!"

*Honey, are you mooning me? Stop. Please do not block my view!*
Did you say honeymoon? "Honey, I can't see anything because of your big lunar. Please get out of the way to allow the stars to align."
"Hey, don't go there until we decide to marry, okay? Your head is way in the clouds, baby. We're not even married yet and you're already planning a honeymoon?" So what's wrong with that, you Big Dipper!

*Do not settle for second best.*
Boys' night out? Girls' night out? "Are we tired of each other already, dear?" Make your spouse a friend, and you'll want to spend more nights together rather than few. Love your boo.

*Keep family members and friends at bay.*
"Baby, we can't tuck your family and friends in our king-size bed too. Sweetheart, you're going to have to push them out on the floor. Sorry, but you can only keep your stuffed animals on the bed." Try solving your own issues and let sleeping bags lie. Huh? Get them out of your "bedness." Sorry, I meant business.

*Keep communication simple.*

How come communication is a big issue in marriages? Both man and woman were able to communicate effortlessly at birth when the doctor slapped their little fanny. They sure did cry. Wail, but do not bail! Effective communication doesn't fail.

"We're doomed. We're staring at this thing, right in the face. We're about to slam smack dead into the wall. Where are the paramedics, the emergency medical technicians? Hurry!"

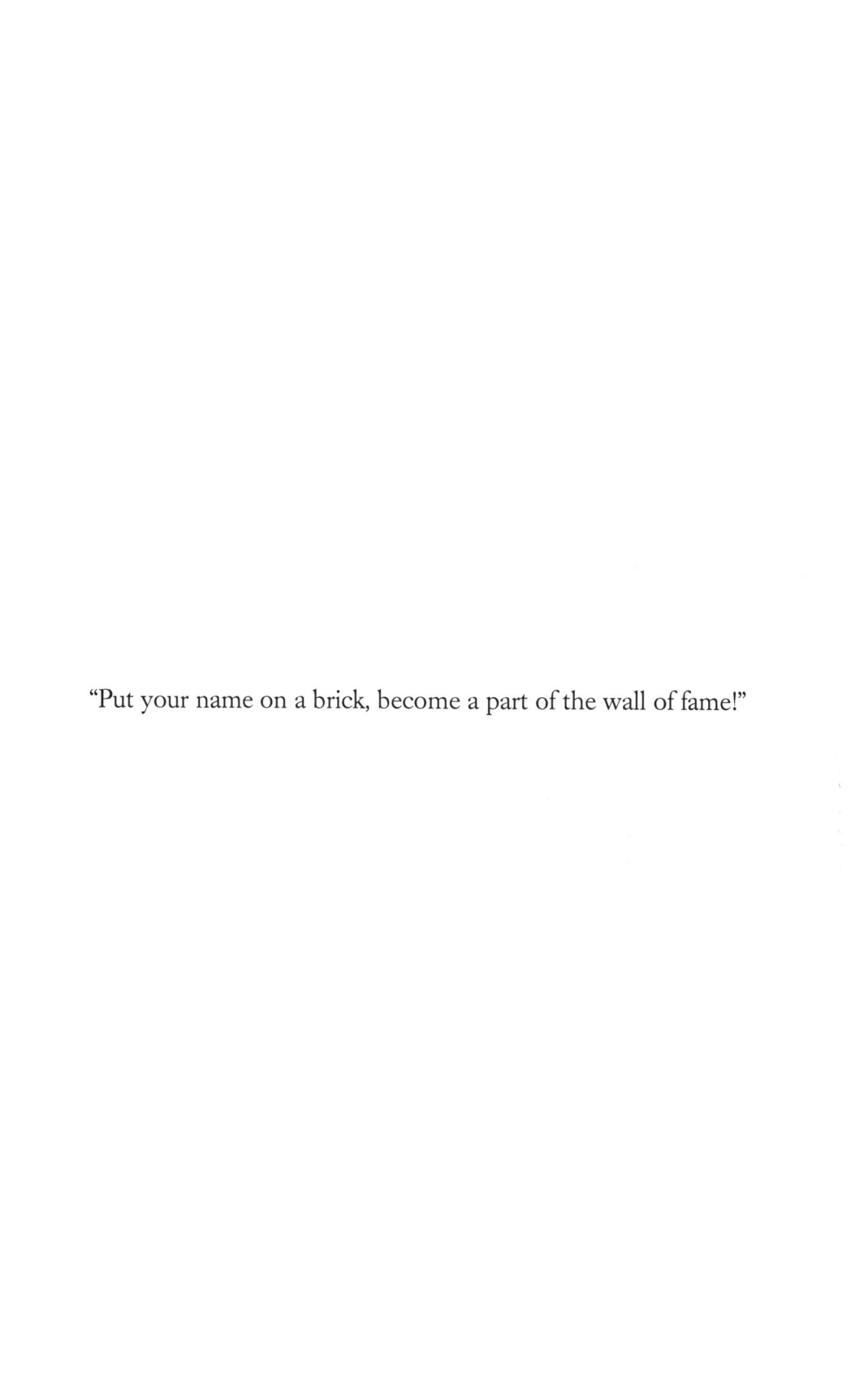

"Put your name on a brick, become a part of the wall of fame!"

# Fastened? Air Bag? Check Check

"Watch out! Watch out! We're getting close to the brick wall! Can you slow down, dear?"

"Need help?"

"I got to make a split-second decision. (Eject!) Oh no."

(Splat.)

"It's your entire fault!"

Another dead end? Emergency vehicles, prepare to enter . . . This scene looks ugly.

*Go to a different cinema and watch a different movie.*
Watch out for the Baby Mama (and Daddy) Drama showing at a theater near you. A box-office smash but causing so much mess in subsequent marriage(s). Starring an ex-spouse who just can't be happy. Get a life, no need for scene one twice!

*Set boundaries. Don't cross that little white line.*
A mind-set of *anything* and *everything* goes in love, war, and marriage won't work either. You can't be all over the map. Move over here to stay. Calm your nerves; quit fidgeting.

*Get help; do not tolerate infidelity.*
Life under the "big top?" The three-ring circus is back in town featuring the cheater (a ferocious cat). His show features a trifecta: ring-off-finger, tan-line-on-finger, and ring-back-on-finger. Wrong. Wrong. Where's the lying tamer?

*Taper your competitiveness.*
Super *S:* soccer mom to the rescue. "My child is more gifted and athletic than your child. He started reading when he was a bun in the oven." Be humble and modest. The world can wait for the next baby Einstein. Let go. Let them have fun.

*Watch your conversations, girls.*
Mom's night is out of sight and lights-out! It's all about "Girl, what from A to Z has happened in your marriage and life today? Let us compare notes." Stop gossiping. Ouch! Are you spewing poisonous venom into your friend's marriage?

Dora the Explorer *is off on a new adventure. Why not you two? There should be a time to turn off the cartoons and watch grown-up stuff.*
A marriage is not just about the child(ren). Remember the spouse that you claim to love? If you don't, you'll have blue's clues.

*Do not allow your marriage to expire.*
Got spoiled milk? "Baby, I saw our wedding picture on a milk carton. Where are we in this marriage? Are we missing and in danger?" Call the authorities to clean up this mess! "Are we spilled milk too? Waaah, baby!"

*Determine what is causing you to stray away.*
Midlife crisis or is it really a void in your life? Do you have a clue? Too late to get out when you're in it to win it. Do not quit. You have to figure this thing out. You have way too much invested not to make the right decision. Grow up the kid inside and your crisis might subside!

*Create quality time together. Maybe get out and see a movie?*
His idea of date night is sleeping and dreaming, creating his own little rated ZZZ movie. Wake up, man. Get up and get innovative. She needs you to set the stage, you great cinematographer.

# MARRIAGE KEYS FOR CRASH-TEST DUMMIES | 93

*Remember your way home.*

"Honey, I'm home. Will you unlock the door? Please. Please." Do not live single while being married. Do not stay out all night by yourself. Remember that you are supposed to be united in holy matrimony.

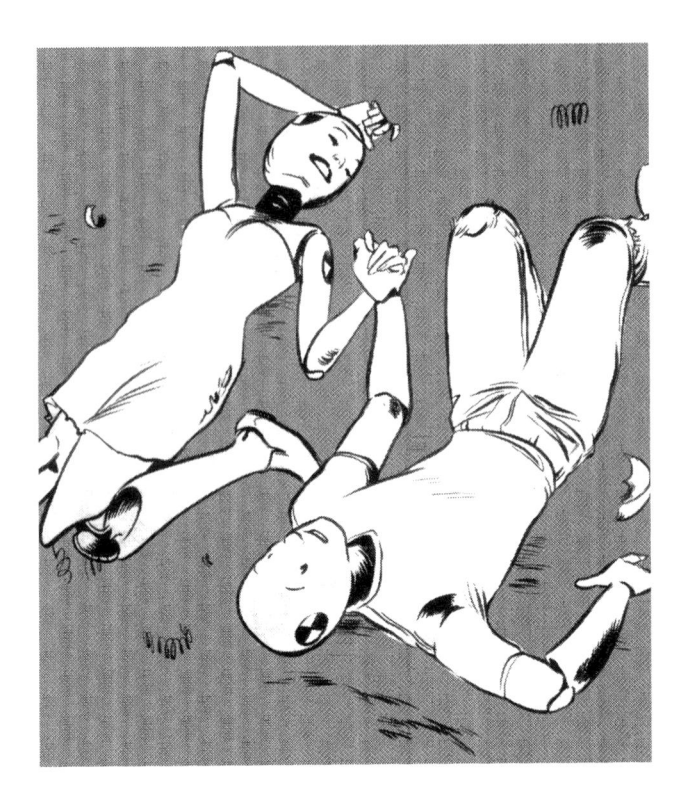

"Baby, are you all right?"

"Yes, I got a few bumps and bruises, but I still love you. Let's try this thing again. We're so much smarter. If we keep charging onward, that brick wall does not have a chance to stand in our way. It will give way!"

*Vroom!*

Moral of this little journey: "Do not let a crash course become a part of your marriage diet!"

"Crash-test dummies, they change and save marriage lives."

# Final Crash-Test Results and Report

Dummies without feathers flock together. Huh? Crashes can be avoided if you don't accompany other dummies to the crash-test site. Do not just go for the ride. Set your own course.

Wait for clear weather to take a spin. Your chances of seeing and avoiding the brick wall vastly improve.

No dummy should drive without a (marriage) license. The divorce judge is looking to take it away if found without it on love's highway.

If you don't misplace your keys, you will not crash. Huh? Go ahead; step into your vehicle and prepare to drive, rookie.

Do not let your dummy (or spouse?) drive drunk. Be his or her designated driver. Somebody has got to have some marriage smarts.

Skid marks are okay if they helped you to avoid a costly crash. Dummies deserve another chance.

Do not try to erase chalked-out lines that outline where bodies landed during the crash test. They give vital information. Did your air bag deploy? If you survived, you can try again.

Dust yourself off. You're okay. Hello, can you hear me? This stuff is invigorating!

Bugs splattered on your windshield do count. They give an indication of your speed and wind direction upon takeoff. Maybe you abort your next crash-test challenge by slowing your acceleration speed.

Bumps and bruises do count for something. Get some medication on those wounds and put that crash helmet back on. Be a survivor.

Ensure that you do get a marriage buggy with a high crash-test rating. You want to "see lots of stars." That means you probably got a decent vehicle. If it rolls over again in an accident, you'll probably come out okay.

Remember, if you ever find your back against the wall, lean on it and look up. Help is on the way! God knows.

Good fortune.

**CROSSWORD PUZZLE**

## *Dummies Don't Cross Words! Will You? Get in the Cross Fire! Huh?*

**Across**

1. This body part requires the action of *26 across* to avoid an argument.
2. Do you date, dummy? Or do you do this? There is a difference. (Hint: the ball is in your _____.)
4. Fight fair even if off balance. Don't try to get _____.
5. To unhappily poke out *1 across*.
11. Your marriage should never end but be _____.
14. Show this in small things, and your love will thrive.
17. You can call your spouse this nickname if he or she isn't scary looking!
18. Like the marines, every marriage is looking for a few good _____.
19. Dummy, your relationship should wear like a new hat, not like an _____ one.
20. A brief love letter penned to your other half. Hint: it's a music symbol.
22. Your spouse should be your _____ mate. Play well and win together.
24. Your marriage shouldn't be _____ afterthought.
26. When communicating with your spouse, it's okay to be in the same jurisdiction or (code).
27. Don't *beat* around the bush; get to the core of the matter.
29. Don't retaliate. No need for tit for _____.
31. Do not take your spouse's energy away. Go get this from a tree instead.
32. A funny new dummy-made dance? Do the _____-trot? (Hint: move your feet and then get yoked together; pull your share of the load, baby.)
33. You _____ boy! You _____ girl! We're good together.
34. My _____-tooth might quicken the pulse of *27 across* if I eat too much chocolate. Join them together and get a clue of you two.
37. It is okay to send this distress smoke signal when your marriage isn't working. (A marriage counselor would be good too.)
38. Dummy partner, you're on fire. Burning! You look smoking after that crash (diet).
39. Let them enhance your marriage, not distract from it. Good parenting skills do help to discipline them.
40. "Zip-a-dee-doo-dah, zip-a-dee-ay, _____ , oh *my*, what a wonderful day!" (Amusing little Song of the South lyrics)
42. You're my _____ in the hole. The best card played.
43. Make up your mind, dummy. Or you _____ are or you out?
44. Maybe is an _____-advised answer.
45. "Born in the _____," Bruce Springsteen sang this song, but are there any successful marriages made here anymore?
47. Woman, are you going to support the house? Are you my _____ or what? Reference *54 across* for support.
48. Every woman wants to be called this.
50. Your spouse wasn't given to you to _____.
51. I don't care how _____ you are. Don't carry that venom to the next day.

**Down**

1. Universal language showing affection.
2. Vital piece of the marriage engine. Don't clog it by being smutty.
3. Your needs are only a _____ of the marital iceberg.
4. You should do this on the side of caution.
6. In marriage, it takes how many, dummy? See, look at these two fingers.
7. "_____ and forever, each moment with you." (Add this hot lyric by the '70s group *Heatwave* to ignite your relationship.)
8. Dummy, you should do this more often than you take.
9. You should listen to your spouse more and not have the gift of this.
10. If you love more, surely you shall receive this badge to signify it.
11. Listen. Your wife might be singing an old Whitney Houston song lyric: "I get so _____, baby."
12. Quit teasing, "_____ already!" (slang phrase?)
13. Sometimes a bitter word to swallow, but if you both succumb to it, your marriage will prosper.
14. Yes, I honor the things you do. I have / or I should have plenty of this for you.
15. If you can't do this, your marriage is as good as dead, dummy! It takes two too. Talk!
16. Opposite of yes? Don't be a pushover all the time. Say this.
17. _____ the odds. Don't let your marriage end in divorce.
21. Don't rock this; don't tip this over because you both might drown, dummy. (Instead, your love should sail like two ships on the ocean. The *Hues Corporation* colored beautifully the lyrics of this '70s song.)
23. This three-letter word sometimes tries to rule the marriage. Don't let it.
25. It is better to live in the corner of an attic than in a house with a wife that does this? Hint: Proverbs 21:9.
27. You're never too old to _____ hands.
28. Harmful toxins in a relationship can act like this chemical abbrev., and it can blow your marriage to pieces.
30. Your spouse should be at the _____ of your priority list.
31. Dummy, drown in a _____ of love for your spouse.
35. He is probably wired like the abbreviation for this form of electrical current. (Careful, don't get your wires crossed.)
36. This should have no place in your marriage. Learn to share. Didn't your parents teach you to not display this type of behavior when you were a kid? Huh?
37. Another name for disgrace. Don't bring this on your marriage.
41. Rhymes with dummy, and when you want something good, it has to be this to your tummy.
46. If you must wrestle, let your spouse win sometimes.
47. Adopt a good theme song for your marriage. Ask Aretha Franklin to tell you what it means.
48. Don't confuse good-_____ with good buy every time you leave home for the shopping mall, dummy.

52. Sometimes it is good to be quiet before a fight develops. Become _____? (It rhymes with hum.)
53. Add an *r* to this if you're going to fight. Go right ahead, dummy. (Also, you might want to give her some of this treatment afterward.)
54. God took out 47 across from Adam and made her. She became a helpmeet for him.
55. Don't talk back, dummy, or be like this, but feel free to dress like this.
57. Divorce shouldn't be an _____ in your marriage.
58. Are you like a light switch? _____ or off? Stay the former.
60. Use this instrument to write *20 across*.
63. If you're divorced, don't let your ex-_____ you. Hint: were you a former prisoner in your marriage?
65. Marriage takes this, dummy. Don't give up. Where is your staying power?
66. Say it. Do you love me or _____?
69. In a marriage, you're but two? Help me, dummy. This doesn't make sense.
70. If your marriage is to thrive, take out _____. It is not a vital part.
72. Do something. For no special reason. Why? "_____."
75. "_____ for nothing or nothing for_____!"
77. If I have to _____ you, you don't need to know. Now that doesn't make sense, dummy?
79. Feels better than a firm mattress. You gotta do this to give your marriage some backbone. Support it.
81. This comes easy when you're giving. Don't be stingy.
82. Sergeant Dummy, report for _____!
84. Some people got to have it; some people really need it.
85. "No _____s, ands, or buts." Just go do it.
86. If you're this, dummy, you won't get *84 across*.
88. Your marriage should be based on _____, not *76 down* (rhyming words).
90. The state of something dead (abbreviation). Besides, let those hurtful words rest in a grave.
91. Coffee, _____, or me. Let it be me!
93. If you can't finish this crossword puzzle, I'll call you this. It takes one to know one. Ha!
95. Don't let your union be "_____ said, she said."
96. In a marriage, you won't land safely flying this way.
98. Diamonds look as cold as this. Hopefully, not you, dummy!
101. If you do *25 down*, you might get called this (an old cranky lady).
102. When proposing, you're asking to do what? "_____ the knot."
104. _____ better or worse, in sickness and health.
106. Send your spouse this kind of package to show your affection.
107. _____ or never.
108. Make your gal your _____ (rhyming words).
109. Feel free to take off the blindfold; you can do it. Pin this on that old donkey.
110. Make your marriage the greatest story ever _____.

49. Killer of *9 down*, opposite of.
50. Remember to set a night periodically with your spouse. It could do wonders for your marriage.
51. Don't let your marriage fall into a state of longtime _____. (Hint: ancient history.)
53. "Say it ain't _____!" (Phrase) Don't shock me.
56. Show her some of this. It will go a long ways. LOL, dummy.
59. "Say my _____, say my _____!" (Song lyrics by Beyonce) At least it would be good to hear it.
60. You two go good together. Like fresh-smelling socks. What are you? A _____.
61. You don't always have to be a freak! Tidy up later. Just relax a little.
62. _____ me halfway. Learn to compromise.
64. When I propose, please say this.
67. Don't wait for tomorrow. Do it now. When?
68. People say that it is the spice of life! Like a smorgasbord, it is good for your marriage too.
70. *Passion of the* _____ (religious movie). Try him in your relationship too.
71. Don't push your marriage off this. And don't make it a hanger either. Have some answers.
73. It is good and all so good to say this when you're wrong, "I'm _____."
74. Remember, don't come home with this on your face.
76. Don't fall into this and mistake it for love.
78. Your marriage should be for good. For how long, dummy?
79. She might be wired like this electric current (abbreviation). *Opposite of 35 down*, the way he be wired.
80. Forever: "We'll be together come whatever _____." (Hint: it's a month, dummy!)
81. Divorce puts your marriage up for _____. And it can be expensive.
83. When you don't understand, dummy, just go "_____?" (A dumb expression.) You might get help.
85. Another word for anger.
87. Give your spouse one of these when he or she is feeling blue. Feel free to rhyme it with mug.
89. _____ the mood. Romantic candles might do.
92. I accept you _____ you are.
93. The first words that your baby might say to get his or her daddy's attention, "Da _____."
94. If you're going to give your spouse a fresh kiss, you might want to pop in one.
97. A little white one never works. Don't get caught up in this tale.
99. Why buy this animal when you can have the milk free? Don't get caught in the barn sitting on a stool. Udder something, dummy!
100. Jump over stylishly. Also a cool partner with *101 down*.
101. Hopefully, you won't need to replace one of these as you age.
103. Don't _____ your way out of your marriage. It can weigh on your partner, dummy.
105. Abbreviation for advertisement. It is okay to create a great one for your marriage.

# Williamson/Marriage/Crossword Puzzle

Dummies are empty sometimes. Huh?

## Williamson/Marriage/Crossword Answers

You can learn a lot from dummies! Huh?

## Answers

# Index

## A

Adam, 25, 100
Adultery, 55
adventure, 4, 7, 9, 91
anomaly, 37
assets, 36, 76

## B

baby Einstein, 90
Bible, 72, 74
bride, 21, 26, 77–78
budget, 78

## C

cart-before-the-horse syndrome, 60
checking accounts, 72
commitment, 24, 37
communication, 57, 85
courtship, 19
creation, 23
creator, 7, 9, 12, 23, 37

## D

danger zone, 35
destination, 29, 37

divorce, 11, 50, 62, 76, 81–82, 96, 99–100
*Dora the Explorer*, 91
dunce cap, 51

## E

Easter, 58
Energizer Bunny, 39
Eve, 25
expectations, 18, 42
expenses, 78

## F

finances, 78
Flattery, 54

## G

God, 23, 25, 34, 97, 100
gofer, 19
goldfish, 40
GPS, 67
gum, 30

## H

holy matrimony, 93
honeymoon, 50, 84

## I

ignition, 31
immaturity, 25
infidelity, 90

## K

key destinations, 15

## L

Lamaze, 34
Liberty Bell, 50
lingerie, 44
loafer, 19

## M

manure, 25
marriage, 15, 19, 22–23, 27–28,
    35, 39–40, 43–45, 49, 51, 62,
    67–70, 72, 74, 76, 94, 96
  healthy, 40
  lovely, 19
  prosperous, 74
  succulent, 27
  unhappy, 11, 70
marriage counseling, 69
marriage engine, 44, 99
marriage health, 35
marriage hideaway, 39
marriage highway, 15
marriage ingredients, 43
marriage institution, 11, 23
marriage interest, 45
marriage landscape, 67
marriage lawn, 68
marriage life, 44
marriage lip-o-suction, 35
marriage math, 51

marriage proposal, 22
marriage roadmap, 15
marriage tune-up, 44
marriage wheel, 28
mind-set, 62, 89
money, 13, 21, 50, 53, 55
money pressures, 18
money problems, 21
morning dew, 41

## N

navigational system, 74

## O

*Off the Wall*, 57
old habits, 64

## P

pettiness, 42
pivotal marital insight, 15
Positive affirmation, 21
positive thinking, 62
Prince Charming, 42

## R

rib, 25, 42
Richie Rich, 18
roadmap, 15
role model, 17

## S

second chances, 21
self-worth, 37
smacks, 40
sports car, 55

## U

unconventional wisdom, 5, 27

## V

vanities, 76

## W

wisdom, 5, 12, 15, 34, 74

Made in the USA
Lexington, KY
25 July 2014